P9-CBC-346

HAMMERED BY HURRICANES

MELISSA RAÉ SHOFNER

Published in 2018 by The Rosen Publishing Group, Inc.
29 East 21st Street, New York, NY 10010

Copyright © 2018 by The Rosen Publishing Group, Inc.

All rights reserved. No part of this book may be reproduced in any form without permission in writing from the publisher, except by a reviewer.

First Edition

Editor: Melissa Raé Shofner
Book Design: Reann Nye

Photo Credits: Cover, p. 1NICOLAS GARCIA/AFP/Getty Images; pp. 4–30 (background) Amanda Clement/Photodisc/Getty Images; pp. 4, 17 Joe Raedle/Getty Images News/Getty Images; p. 5 OLI SCARFF/AFP/Getty Images; p. 6 Win McNamee/Getty Images News/Getty Images; p. 7 Mike Theiss/ National Geographic/Getty Images; pp. 9, 13 Stocktrek Images/Getty Images; p. 11 Pasha_Barabanov/ Shutterstock.com; p. 15 Dave Einsel/Getty Images News/Getty Images; p. 19 PAUL J. RICHARDS/AFP/ Getty Images; p. 20 Franz Marc Frei/Corbis Documentary/Getty Images; pp. 21, 25 STAN HONDA/ AFP/Getty Images; p. 23 William Thomas Cain/Getty Images News/Getty Images; p. 24 Jim Edds/ Science Source/Getty Images; p. 26 Win McNamee/Getty Images News/Getty Images; p. 27 Mario Tama/Getty Images News/Getty Images; p. 29 Yann Arthus-Bertrand/Getty Images.

Cataloging-in-Publication Data

Names: Shofner, Melissa Raé.
Title: Hammered by hurricanes / Melissa Raé Shofner.
Description: New York : PowerKids Press, 2018. | Series: Natural disasters: how people survive | Includes index.
Identifiers: LCCN ISBN 9781538326305 (pbk.) | ISBN 9781538325612 (library bound) | ISBN 9781538326312 (6 pack)
Subjects: LCSH: Hurricanes–Juvenile literature.
Classification: LCC QC944.2 S56 2018 | DDC 363.34'922–dc23

Manufactured in the United States of America

CPSIA Compliance Information: Batch #BW18PK: For Further Information contact Rosen Publishing, New York, New York at 1-800-237-9932

CONTENTS

NATURE'S WRATH 4

THE RIGHT CONDITIONS 6

EYE OF THE STORM 8

HURRICANE SEASON 10

GROWING STRONGER 12

MEASURING HURRICANES 14

STORM TECH 16

ISSUING A WARNING 18

STAY OR EVACUATE? 20

PREPARE FOR THE WORST 22

DURING THE STORM 24

OTHER DANGERS 26

AFTER A HURRICANE 28

HURRICANE SAFETY TIPS 30

GLOSSARY 31

INDEX 32

WEBSITES 32

NATURE'S WRATH

Natural disasters are events in nature that cause great destruction in populated areas. They may also cause many deaths. Earthquakes and blizzards are two types of natural disasters. You may have heard about these events in the news.

Hurricanes are also natural disasters. These violent storms may be hundreds of miles wide, bringing strong winds and heavy rains to large areas. To make matters

DISASTER ALERT!

Spanish explorers used the word *huracán* to refer to the terrible storms that sank their ships in the Caribbean. A native people of the Caribbean used a similar word for the name of their god of evil.

According to the National Weather Service, hurricanes are intense, or very strong, **tropical** weather systems with strong circular motion and steady wind speeds of 74 miles (119.1 km) per hour or greater.

worse, hurricanes also cause other natural disasters such as flooding and tornadoes.

Recent improvements in **technology** have made it easier to **predict** when and where hurricanes will hit. This has led to better warning systems, which have helped save many lives. Still, knowing how to stay safe during a hurricane is very important if you live in or travel to an area where these powerful storms occur.

THE RIGHT CONDITIONS

Hurricanes are known for high winds, heavy rains, and low atmospheric pressure. They form near the equator, where they get energy from warm ocean waters. As wind moves over the ocean, warm water evaporates, or turns to vapor. This water vapor rises and cools, forming tall clouds and large raindrops. This rising warm air creates a low-pressure area near the ocean's

DISASTER ALERT!

For a hurricane to form, at least the top 164 feet (50 m) of water beneath the ocean's surface must be 80° Fahrenheit (26.7° C) or warmer.

Hurricanes continue to gain strength as they travel across tropical waters. However, they quickly weaken as they make their way inland or move into colder waters.

surface. Cool air pushes in to replace it, then warms and rises as well.

Trouble begins when the air around the low-pressure area begins to move in a fast **spiral**. Warm, wet ocean air continues to be sucked up and carried out and over the storm, which causes wind speeds to increase. Faster winds create lower air pressure at the center of the storm, and the pattern continues.

7

EYE OF THE STORM

The winds of a hurricane swirl, or spin, around a main area of low pressure. This center area of a hurricane is called the eye. Surprisingly, the air within the eye of a hurricane is calm and cloudless.

If you're caught in a hurricane, don't be fooled by the calm conditions of the eye of the storm. The most dangerous part of the hurricane—the eyewall—will hit again soon. As its name suggests, the eyewall of a hurricane surrounds the eye. The strongest winds and heaviest rains are found here.

Rainbands are long bands of thunderstorm clouds that spiral inward toward the center of a hurricane. Rainbands bring bursts of rain and wind with calmer gaps between bands. Wind speeds decrease as you move farther out from the eye.

DISASTER ALERT!

As if one natural disaster isn't enough to worry about, tornadoes sometimes form within the rainbands of a hurricane.

Satellite images clearly showed the different parts of Hurricane Matthew as it slammed into the Florida coast on October 7, 2016.

eye wall

eye

rainbands

HURRICANE
SEASON

Scientists use the term "tropical cyclone" to refer to hurricane-like storms around the world. These systems go by different names depending on where they form. When they form over the eastern Pacific or Atlantic Ocean, these systems are called hurricanes. When they form in the South Pacific or Indian Ocean, they're called cyclones. When these systems form in the western North Pacific Ocean or near the Philippines, they're called typhoons.

The Atlantic hurricane season runs from June 1 until November 30 each year. This is when the greatest number of hurricanes form in this area. The peak of the Atlantic hurricane season is between mid-August and late October. If you plan to travel somewhere tropical during hurricane season, definitely keep an eye on the weather.

More than 12 hurricanes form on average each year over the Atlantic Ocean. These storms move west toward eastern Central America, the Caribbean, and the southern United States, feeding off the warm ocean water as they go.

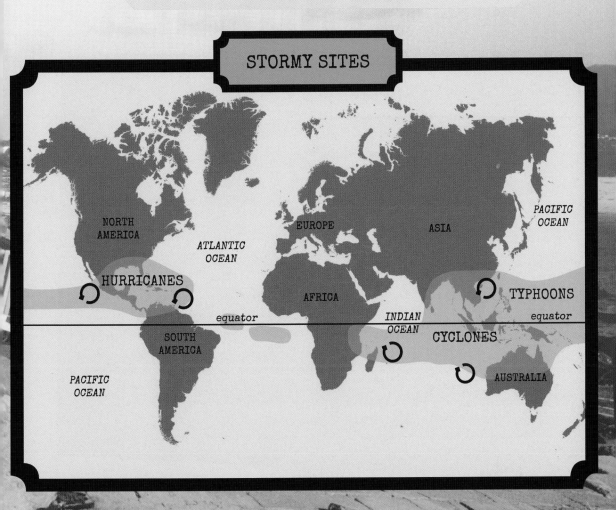

STORMY SITES

NORTH AMERICA

ATLANTIC OCEAN

EUROPE

ASIA

PACIFIC OCEAN

HURRICANES

AFRICA

equator

INDIAN OCEAN

TYPHOONS

equator

SOUTH AMERICA

CYCLONES

PACIFIC OCEAN

AUSTRALIA

The Coriolis Effect

GROWING STRONGER

Before becoming a hurricane, a storm system begins as a tropical disturbance. Tropical disturbances occur when clouds begin to organize and show slight circulation, or spinning motion. If a disturbance continues to organize and grow stronger, it may become a tropical depression. Tropical depressions have winds that swirl at speeds between 25 and 38 miles (40.2 and 61.2 km) per hour.

If a storm system continues to strengthen, it may become a tropical storm. Tropical storms have wind speeds from 39 to 73 miles (62.8 and 117.5 km) per hour. At this stage, winds begin to swirl around a developed eye and a storm is given a name. When wind speeds

DISASTER ALERT!

Typhoon Tip hit Japan on October 10, 1979. At its largest, it

This satellite image shows Hurricane Irene moving across the Bahamas on August 25, 2011. Irene stretched about 510 miles (820.8 km) across and was about 1/3 the size of the East Coast.

Collecting Data

The United States is the only country that uses aircraft to directly observe hurricanes as they form. These aircraft use a special device called a dropsonde to collect data about the temperature, wind speed, **humidity**, and atmospheric pressure within a storm system.

MEASURING HURRICANES

When tropical storms in the eastern Pacific or Atlantic Ocean reach hurricane strength, scientists measure their top wind speed and possible storm surge in order to issue suitable warnings. The storm surge is when seawater rises and is pushed onto the land by fierce winds. The storm surge may be as high as 20 feet (6.1 m), which means flooding is a huge danger. In the United States, about half of the deaths that occur when a hurricane makes landfall are due to storm surge.

After measuring the intensity of a hurricane, scientists use a special system called the Saffir-Simpson scale to rank the storm. The Saffir-Simpson scale places hurricanes into five categories based on their top wind speed and storm surge. Category 1 hurricanes result in little damage, while category 5 hurricanes are **catastrophic**.

DISASTER ALERT!

The Galveston, Texas, hurricane of 1900 is the deadliest storm in U.S. history. Between 8,000 and 12,000 people were killed. Around 6,000 of these deaths were caused by the 15-foot (4.6 m) storm surge.

CATEGORY	WIND SPEED	DAMAGE AT LANDFALL
1	74–95 MPH (119.1–152.9 KMH)	MINIMAL
2	96–110 MPH (154.5–177 KMH)	MODERATE
3	111–130 MPH (178.6–209.2 KMH)	EXTENSIVE
4	131–155 MPH (210.8–249.4 KMH)	EXTREME
5	> 155 MPH (> 249.4 KMH)	CATASTROPHIC

A category 3 hurricane may cause more deaths and greater destruction than a category 5 hurricane if it directly hits a heavily populated area. The true impact, or effect, of a hurricane depends on the area where it makes landfall.

Beware of Water

Hurricanes are ranked by the speed of their winds, but it's actually the water associated with a hurricane that does the most damage. The National Hurricane Center (NHC) has reported that 88 percent of deaths in the United States from tropical depressions, tropical storms, and hurricanes between 1963 and 2012 were water related. High surf, storm surge, and flooding due to rainfall can be very deadly during a hurricane.

STORM TECH

Forecasting where and when a hurricane will make landfall is much easier today than in the past. For a long time, people had to observe changes in the weather and the surface of the ocean using just their senses. They also relied on reports from areas where a hurricane had already hit.

Today, **meteorologists** use modern technology to make faster, more precise hurricane predictions. This means warnings can be issued sooner and more lives may be saved.

Weather satellites, which were first used in the 1960s, provide a view of Earth from space. They allow meteorologists to view changes in clouds that can indicate the formation of a hurricane as well as its strength. Satellite images are also used to track a hurricane's path and make predictions about where it will make landfall.

The National Hurricane Center is located in Miami, Florida. Its mission is to issue better hurricane forecasts and warnings in an attempt to lessen property damage and save lives.

Long-Term Forecasts

Meteorologists can now create long-term forecasts before the beginning of each year's hurricane season. To do this, they closely study the wind, rain, atmospheric pressure, and ocean conditions in different parts of the world. Meteorologists use this data to make predictions about the number and intensity of tropical storms and tropical cyclones that will hit the Atlantic region during the upcoming hurricane season. Long-term forecasts are first issued in December, then revised in June and August.

ISSUING A WARNING

NHC meteorologists track hurricanes carefully. If they believe a coastal area may experience hurricane conditions within 36 hours, they issue a hurricane watch for that area. Meteorologists use computer models and other observation methods to make a "best track" forecast. This is their best guess about where a hurricane will move and what speed its winds will peak at over a 72-hour period.

A warning may be issued if a hurricane is expected to hit an area within 24 hours. At this point, people are urged to leave areas where storm surge and flooding are known to occur and head to higher ground. Sometimes, emergency officials will call for a mandatory, or required, evacuation of an area. This means everyone must leave right away.

DISASTER ALERT!

When a tropical depression forms, the NHC issues and updates an advisory at least every six hours. The advisory may become a watch or a warning as the system strengthens and moves closer to land.

Large hurricanes aren't always the strongest. Smaller hurricanes can pack a punch, too. Hurricane Andrew hit south Florida in 1992 with winds up to 175 miles (281.6 km) per hour, causing severe damage across a strip of land only 40 miles (64.4 km) wide.

Naming Hurricanes

The NHC has given tropical storms in the Atlantic Ocean names since 1953. A storm keeps its name if it strengthens into a hurricane. This helps people keep track of them, which is especially important when multiple storms are developing at once. The NHC has created six lists of alternating male and female names. If a hurricane causes major death and destruction, its name may be permanently removed from the list and a new name will be added.

STAY OR EVACUATE?

If a hurricane warning is issued for your area, you must decide if you want to evacuate or stay and ride out the storm. In places where a hurricane is expected to cause great damage, a mandatory evacuation may be issued in an effort to protect the lives of residents and emergency personnel. Some people choose to ignore mandatory evacuation notices. This can be very dangerous, especially because rescuers may not risk their

DISASTER ALERT!

Whether you decide to stay or leave during a hurricane, it's important to plan ahead. Shop for necessary supplies before a warning is issued. Otherwise, stores may be sold out of items or closed.

If your family needs to evacuate, they should do so immediately. Let someone who is out of the hurricane's path know your plan. You don't need to travel far—just a safe distance outside the evacuation zone.

lives responding to emergency calls in these areas when the hurricane hits.

Places where hurricanes are common often have certain roads and highways marked as evacuation routes. Be aware of these routes and have an evacuation plan ready in case you need to leave in a hurry. You should also have a backup plan and a plan for your pets.

PREPARE FOR THE WORST

Before a hurricane hits, there are a few things you can do to protect your home, your belongings, and your family. The first and most important step is having a plan and putting it into action. You should have an emergency supply kit with items to help you get by for a few days without electricity or running water. This kit should contain clean drinking water, food that won't spoil, a first-aid kit, medications, flashlights, a battery-powered radio, and extra batteries. It's also a good idea to make copies of important paperwork, such as **insurance** documents.

Tune in to news reports about the approaching hurricane. Hurricanes sometimes change course, and it may be safer for you to move to a shelter if your home is suddenly in the storm's direct path.

DISASTER ALERT!

Remember to secure or bring inside any objects on your property that might blow away. Remove any damaged branches from trees in your yard, and check to be sure your roof and rain **gutters** are in working order.

Sheets of wood called plywood may be used to cover doors and windows before a hurricane hits. Be safe and board up your home early. It can be difficult and dangerous to handle sheets of plywood once the wind picks up.

Boarding Up

DURING
THE STORM

Hurricanes can be very scary, but staying calm and following safety measures can help you survive. When a hurricane hits, you should stay inside and keep away from windows. The safest place in a house is an interior room, such as a bathroom or closet, on the lowest level. If the electricity goes out, don't light candles. They could be knocked over and may start a fire.

The most intense hurricanes may have sustained wind speeds of 150 miles (241.4 km) per hour. Wind gusts may be more than 200 miles (321.9 km) per hour. These strong winds may last for hours depending on how big a storm is and how fast it's moving.

Remember that the eyewall of a hurricane is where the strongest winds and rains are found. Don't go outside when the eye of the hurricane passes over your area and the weather clears up. The weather will get bad again soon, and you could become stuck outside during the worst part of the storm.

OTHER DANGERS

There are many dangers associated with hurricanes, including strong winds and heavy rains. Some places may receive 20 to 40 inches (50.8 to 101.6 cm) of rain during a hurricane. This, along with the storm surge, can cause terrible flooding. Floodwaters can pollute drinking water, sweep away vehicles, spread disease, and cause dangerous mold growth.

DISASTER ALERT!

Hurricane Harvey, a category 4 storm, hit the Gulf Coast of Texas on August 25, 2017. Harvey dumped about 19 trillion gallons (71.9 trillion L) of rain on southeast Texas in less than a week. Some parts of Texas received more than 50 inches (127 cm) of rain.

A huge fire broke out in Breezy Point, New York, after Hurricane Sandy hit the area on October 29, 2012. The fire destroyed more than 80 homes.

Tornadoes may also form in a hurricane's rainbands, creating additional problems for areas already dealing with extreme weather. If a hurricane produces tornadoes, there are usually fewer than 10. Some, however, have many more. In 1967, Hurricane Beulah hit the Gulf Coast of Texas and produced 141 tornadoes.

Downed electrical lines can be dangerous, especially if water is nearby. Broken gas lines may cause fires. Without power, it's often difficult to contact rescuers and emergency officials.

27

AFTER A HURRICANE

Pay attention to the news reports about a hurricane to know when the storm is over. It may be unsafe to go outside until the hurricane has completely passed over your area. The destruction after a hurricane can be overwhelming. Try to remain calm and have patience. It might be a while before things are back to normal. Be on the lookout for downed electrical lines. Report any you see, and stay away from them.

It may be unsafe to drink tap water for some time after a hurricane. Drink the bottled water in your emergency supply until officials say the taps are safe again. Avoid walking or driving through floodwaters as they may contain dangerous debris or diseases.

Floodwaters are the leading cause of hurricane-related deaths.

DISASTER ALERT!

Rescue and relief efforts are often provided by organizations such as the Red Cross, UNICEF, and the National Guard. These groups bring clean water, food, and other supplies to victims after natural disasters. They may also help towns and cities rebuild.

28

Hurricane Katrina damaged much of the Gulf Coast area of the United States in late August 2005. More than 20 percent of the city of New Orleans, Louisiana, was under water due to heavy rains and storm surge. Katrina caused more than $100 billion in damages, making it the costliest hurricane in U.S. history.

HURRICANE SAFETY TIPS

Hurricanes can create scary and dangerous situations. Being prepared for one of these natural disasters will help you stay calm and safe.

Follow these tips to stay safe:

- Have an evacuation plan in place before a hurricane hits.

- Assemble an emergency supply kit.

- Board up the windows of your home.

- Secure or bring inside any outdoor items that could blow away.

- Make sure your car has a full tank of gas.

- If you live in a low-lying area, move to a shelter on higher ground.

- Stay indoors unless instructed to evacuate the area.

- Don't walk or drive in floodwater.

- Don't go outside until emergency officials say it's safe

GLOSSARY

barrier island: A long, sandy island that's parallel to the coast.

catastrophic: Causing sudden great damage.

gutter: A device attached beneath the edge of a roof to carry away rainwater.

humidity: The amount of moisture in the air.

insurance: An agreement in which a person pays a company for money in case of damage, illness, or death.

meteorologist: Someone who studies weather, climate, and the atmosphere.

nutrient: Something taken in by a plant or animal that helps it grow and stay healthy.

predict: To guess what will happen in the future based on facts or knowledge.

satellite: A spacecraft placed in orbit around Earth, a moon, or a planet to collect information or for communication.

spiral: A shape or line that curls outward from a center point.

technology: A method that uses science to solve problems and the tools used to solve those problems.

tropical: Having to do with an area of the world known for warm and wet weather.

INDEX

A
Atlantic Ocean, 10, 11, 14, 19

B
Bahamas, 13, 26
Breezy Point, 27

C
Caribbean, 4, 11
Central America, 11
Coriolis effect, 11
Cuba, 26
cyclones, 10, 11, 12, 17

E
equator, 6, 11
eye, 8, 9, 12, 25
eyewall, 8, 9, 25

F
Florida, 9, 17, 19

G
Galveston, 14
Gulf Coast, 27, 29

H
Hurricane Andrew, 19
Hurricane Beulah, 27
Hurricane Irene, 13
Hurricane Katrina, 29
Hurricane Matthew, 9
Hurricane Sandy, 26, 27

I
Indian Ocean, 10, 11

J
Jamaica, 26
Japan, 12

L
Louisiana, 29

M
meteorologists, 16, 17, 18
Miami, 17

N
National Hurricane Center (NHC), 15, 17, 18, 19
National Weather Service, 5
New Jersey, 26
New Orleans, 29
New York, 26, 27

P
Pacific Ocean, 10, 11, 14
Philippines, 10

R
rainbands, 8, 9, 26

S
Saffir-Simpson scale, 14, 15
storm surge, 14, 15, 18, 26, 29

T
Texas, 14, 27
tornadoes, 5, 8, 26, 27
tropical depression, 12, 15, 18
tropical disturbance, 12
tropical storm, 12, 14, 15, 17, 19
typhoons, 10, 11, 12

U
United States, 11, 14, 15, 16, 29

WEBSITES

Due to the changing nature of Internet links, PowerKids Press has developed an online list of websites related to the subject of this book. This site is updated regularly. Please use this link to access the list: www.powerkidslinks.com/natd/hurr